MARCO RYAN

An Insider's 2024 Guide to Florence

Discover the Authentic Florence: Handpicked Activities, Churches, Markets and Hotels, coupled with the Finest Cafés, Bars, and Restaurants Favored by Locals

Pownall
Publishing

Contents

1

INTRODUCTION

I fell in love with Florence or *Firenze* at first sight. I don't know whether it was the imposing public squares, the magnificence of the Duomo, the bustle on the Ponte Vecchio, the first time I dipped a *Cantuccini* into *Vin Santo* or just a sense of being in the heart of Italy, but I was immediately smitten.

Over the last 30 years, I have continued that love affair - coming to Florence to study Italian, to work, and even to get married. I have made life-long friends and come to discover a hidden Florence - one that few tourists see - but that has given me an appreciation and enduring love for the city, its people, and its way of life. This is a city that subtly adapts to modern life whilst remaining at its heart a monument to culture, art, fantastic food, wine, and a passion for life.

Florence has a mystique to it. Over the centuries, it has remained home to poets, writers, artists, and lovers. It is a city of history, engineering brilliance, architecture, and culture. UNESCO recognised its historical significance by awarding the old city centre or *centro storico*, World Heritage status. Unsurprisingly, it is a city visited by about 13 million tourists each year and yet inhabited by only 361,000 locals.

Whether it is the elegance of the shops on the Via de' Tornabuoni, the view over the city from Fiesole, the early morning rowers gliding effortlessly under the Ponte Vecchio, backlit by the rising sun, the strength and delicacy of Michelangelo's Davide or the simple pleasure of sitting outside a cafe sipping a perfect cappuccino whilst watching the world go by....whatever it is that acts as the catalyst, I defy you not to come to Florence and to *feel* the effect it has on you.

Each time I visit Florence, I discover something new. Well, in most cases, I am discovering something ancient but new to me. It might be a hidden courtyard, a new restaurant, a piece of history etched (literally in some cases) on a wall or a new boutique. Florence is a generous city that always offers something new, something familiar and worth returning for.

For years, friends and families have asked for things to do, for restaurant recommendations or insider tips on discovering the real Florence. This book is an attempt to condense some of that knowledge and experiences and collate them in a format that is easier to share and update. I also want to share my enthusiasm and love for a city that has brought me so much happiness and to encourage others - you in this case - to experience the same love for such a fantastic city.

HOW TO USE THIS GUIDE

There are many guidebooks that will help you navigate around the city or provide you with the historical context and details of a particular church or museum. They are superbly researched and photographed and should be in your backpack. But this book is less that type of guide and more of a companion.

It is designed for you to dip into. Sure, you can read it front to back, but it works just as well when you dip in and out, driven by a particular interest or need. Perhaps you want to visit a market but are unsure why one is better than the other. Perhaps you want to escape the crowds of tourists and find the restaurants that the locals go to. Maybe you want to immerse yourself more in the food, the wine, or the culture, but rather than just looking at something as part of a tour, you want to really experience it by *doing it.* Perhaps you are looking for a quiet bar to have an *aperitivo* with friends or a nightclub to really let your hair down. Whatever your need and whatever your mood, I hope that this book will provide you with that sense of discovery.

PRE-PLANNING

Part of the joy of Florence is to be spontaneous. But the large number of tourists packed into a mediaeval walled city means that some things really need to be planned. Much will depend on what time of year you visit - my favourites are May and September, and I always avoid August, which is the peak tourist season. Most Italians shut up their shops and escape to the seaside for the whole of August, so much of the hidden gems mentioned in the book may well be closed if you are brave enough to visit then.

Of course, you should book your accommodation ahead of time. The smaller, more exclusive, or more popular hotels, hostels and Airbnb do tend to get booked months in advance.

Florence is small - certainly by other international cities' standards, and you will be amazed at how quickly you can traverse the city. Most things are within a 20−30-minute walk of the Duomo, so wherever you stay they are accessible.

Bring a comfortable pair of walking shoes. Most of the historic centre is closed to traffic, so everybody, including the locals, walks. The traditional guidebooks or a simple internet search will tell you how to get from the airport (Pisa or Florence) by train, bus, or taxi to where you are staying. (Hint: take the train from Pisa and a bus or Taxi from Florence!)

In terms of restaurant booking, most restaurants can be booked up to a day or so in advance, and most offer online booking. The activity to be prepared to book, though, is a visit to the Uffizi or to climb up to the top of the Duomo. These must be pre-booked. There are also options to book "Skip the line" tours, but more on those later.

2

THE BEST NEIGHBOURHOODS AND WHY

F lorence is divided into five administrative districts, but within that, several smaller and distinct neighbourhoods span the northern and southern sides of the river Arno. They differ significantly in style and purpose, so I thought it would be helpful to give you a little sense of their differences. To the north of the Arno, the main neighbourhoods of note are:

San Giovani

The San Giovanni neighbourhood is at the heart of Florence's historic centre (Centro Storico), which is home to the Duomo. It takes its name from the Baptistery of San Giovani. The Duomo, or the Cathedral of Santa Maria del Fiore to give it its full title, was designed by Filippo Bruneschelli in the 15th Century and is perhaps the most identifiable of Florence's landmarks. Alongside the Duomo is Giotto's Campanile. Around the Duomo, the streets radiate out into the heart of Florence and promise a multitude of shops, restaurants, hotels and markets.

Santa Maria Novella

If you arrive by train, this is the neighbourhood you will arrive in, and it is to the west of the Duomo. It is dominated by the famous square, Piazza di Santa Maria Novella, which takes its name from the impressive church at one end. It is flanked by restaurants and hotels, where you can enjoy an al fresco meal. Pickpockets can be a challenge here, partly due to the vicinity of the train station. Via dei Fossi and Via del Moro have beautiful antique and porcelain shops, and nearby is the world-famous Perfume maker, Officina Profumo Farmaceutica di Santa Maria Novella. If you are hungry, then the wonderful Trattoria Sostanza is a good bet.

Santa Croce

Santa Croce often feels like the cultural heart of Florence, and it is referred to as the "green lung" of the city due to its parks. Situated to the east of San Giovani, it is home to the much-visited Basilica di Santa Croce, a 13th Century church that now houses the tombs of Florence's most famous sons: Michelangelo, Galileo, and Machiavelli. It was also the main district for leather goods, and one of the original leather schools - Scuola Di Cuoio - remains within the cloisters of the Basilica. The cobbled streets of the neighbourhood's many bars and restaurants, with Via dei Benci being a great place to people watch, as there is a mix of artisan, professional and tourist in the streets, many cafes and bars. At night this street seems to be full of students soaking up the atmosphere

San Lorenzo

To the North of San Giovani, is the recently gentrified neighbourhood of San Lorenzo. Initially one of the poorer market areas, the recent refurbishment of the Mercato Centrale into a major food destination, together with the vibrant street markets (see section on <u>markets</u>) around Via dell'Ariento during the day selling all manner of tourist goods, clothes and leather makes it one of Florence's most popular neighbourhoods. At night, the vibrancy continues with great bars and restaurants such as Sabor Cubano and la Ménagère.

A quick sidebar, though, on counterfeit goods. NEVER, and I mean NEVER, be tempted to buy one, even for a friend. It is illegal to sell or buy counterfeit goods. There is zero tolerance from the police, with fines up to €10,000, and even your embassy or consulate cannot help. It simply isn't worth it.

Sant' Ambrogio

Further East from Sant Croce is a neighbourhood that has few tourists and oozes local charm. The fruit and vegetable markets (see section on <u>markets</u>) are an ideal way to mix with the locals, including many of the chefs from the neighbouring restaurants who get their fresh ingredients in the same markets. If you are feeling peckish, then Trattoria L'Ortone is a cave-like tavern with both underground and street-level tables serving delicious local Tuscan dishes. If it's passing the time of day over a lazy cappuccino, then either Caffè Sant'Ambrogio, where you sit beside pensioners and students alike, or Cibréo Caffè with its sun-kissed terrace.

To the south side of the Arno (or *Oltrano*) are:

Santo Spirito

This hip neighbourhood on the south side of the Arno has an eclectic mix of students, locals, and businesses. The bustling Piazza Santo Spirito boasts some amazing trattorias. One of my favourite places for a Cappuccino and a chat with the locals is the tiny Pop Cafe. The neighbouring streets are home to many of the artisan workshops, and Via di Santo Spirito boasts multiple wine shops and enoteca. If antiques are more your thing, then Via Maggio has lots to offer, but of course, you can see the real thing in the nearby and impressive Palazzo Pitti, which is also bordered by the stunning and formal Boboli Gardens.

San Frediano

Just across the Ponte Vecchio and on the Oltrano side of the Arno is San Frediano. The boutiques full of leather and fashion soon give way to small streets full of old-style trattorias and osteria serving simple Tuscan food. Like San Lorenzo, it has recently become more gentrified, and what were workshops or small stores have given way to restaurants and bars. Stanley Tucci, in his recent TV series, loved the Osteria Cinghiale Bianco. Memorable Pizza can be found at Pizza Tasso, and a good set lunch option is L'Brindellone. One of the best places to stay (budget permitting) is the Lungarno Hotel which has breath-taking views of the Ponte Vecchio and a fun little balcony cafe where you can bask in the sunlight.

San Niccolo

The smallest of the neighbourhoods but regarded as the modern creative zone, its streets are lined with galleries and studios, and it is one of the last places where you can see and touch the original mediaeval walls of the city. The neighbourhood comes to life around *aperitivo* time, with every corner seeming to boast a bustle of tables, chairs and locals talking with expanded hand gestures. If you want to be brave, try the Tripe with Basil when you dine in the old crypt at the nineteenth-century Osteria Antica Mescita.

or alternatively, go to Beppa Fioraia, a cosy trattoria full of locals.

3

THE BEST PLACES TO VISIT

THE BEST CHURCHES

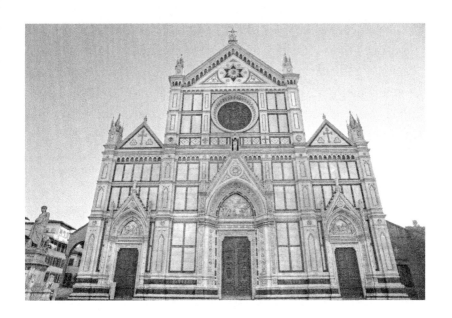

I have deliberately excluded the Duomo from this list for several reasons. Although it is an extraordinary masterpiece of architecture, engineering, opulence, and grandeur, you must be prepared to queue. If you want to climb the stairs to the very top, be sure to plan and buy a ticket. I love the Duomo, but I think there are so many other hidden treasures in churches around Florence that so few visitors ever go and see that it is worth just shining the briefest of lights on them.

Basilica Santa Croce

This is one of the most important churches in Florence, partly because of who is interred here but also because of some of the art and frescoes on its walls and ceilings. It was begun in the early 13th century and is still the largest Franciscan Church in the world, with some claiming that St. Francis himself may have founded it. It wasn't consecrated until 1142, when Brunelleschi finished the Pazzi Family chapel. Inside are 16 chapels, funded by the wealthy families of the time, and ornately frescoed by Giotto. Some stunning and important Crucifixes include Donatello's Farmer's Crucifix and Cimabue's Crucifix from 1280. It is also the resting place of some of Florence's greatest sons - Michelangelo, Galileo, Machiavelli, and Rossini. Dante - Florence's other great son famed for the Divine Comedy" and its impact on the Italian language - still lies in Ravenna, so the sarcophagus in the Basilica Santa Croce is empty.

Santa Maria Novella

The striped marble facade, which was completed in 1470, is original. It was a mark of wealth to place a facade on the front of the church built by Dominican friars between 1279 and 1370. Inside, the church is enormous, with a nave about 100m/300ft long, but its real secret is the unique art it contains. There are crucifixes by Brunelleschi and Giotto, frescoes by Lippi, Allori and Ghirlandaio and a host of important paintings. The cloisters are also peaceful and partly frescoed.

Chiesa di Ognissanti

This is an important church for several reasons. Firstly, it is a baroque church built in the 17th Century on top of an old mediaeval church. Secondly, it houses some of the finest frescoes painted by Ghirlandaio and Botticelli (who is buried there), and in the refectory of the church is Ghirlandaio's Last Supper, which was painted in 1480. But perhaps most importantly, the church always seems to be empty and is the perfect antidote to a city crowded with tourists.

Santa Trinità

Dating back to the eleventh century, this church has undergone several improvements and enlargements over the centuries. Inside are 20 family chapels, including the Sassetti chapel that houses some of Ghirlandaio's best fresco work. The Doni Chapel with frescoes by Bicci di Lorenzo and the Spini Chapel are also worthy of note.

Santo Spirito

The church forms one side of this Piazza, which is full of cafes and eateries, and two weekends a month, it also holds an outdoor market. It is an unassuming church, one of the last to be designed by Brunelleschi. It is an ordered church - with precise geometry, and its columns, mouldings, and cornices are in the local grey-green marble. Of note is Michelangelo's Crucifix - carved by the artist when he was just 17 and as payment for his free study of anatomy and bodies, which gave him such an in-depth knowledge of anatomy. It is hung from the ceiling. It is impressive and worth seeing.

Santa Felicita'

This was brought to my attention by Corinna Cooke in her excellent guide. I never knew it existed. Technically one of Florence's oldest churches (though rebuilt in the Mediaeval and Renaissance periods), it is notable for two things. Inside its Capponi Chapel is a Pontorno painting called "The Deposition". I won't steal Corinna's thunder, but it is worth a look. The second remarkable thing about this church is that the Vasari Corridor (that links the Palazzo Vecchio and the Pitti Palace and meant that the nobles did not have to walk on the street or across the Ponte Vecchio with the masses) has a secret passageway and grate into the church.

Basilica San Miniato al Monte

This is a short step from Piazzale Michelangelo. Perhaps most remarkable about San Minato is its facade - one of the best-preserved examples of the striped grey and green marble later copied in Santa Croce and Santa Maria Novella. Inside is special, too. A painted wooden ceiling, 800-year-old frescoes on the walls and marble panels on the floor and, as it is still a functioning church, you might even hear the monks chanting.

Basilica San Lorenzo

Arguably one of the most important churches in Florence and possibly the oldest, it came into being under the Medici, who used it as their family Church. Designed by Brunelleschi but with colossal bronze doors by Donatello, it boasts so much culture and art that it requires its own book. Make sure to see Michelangelo's staircase - reputedly the first free-standing staircase in the world - Michelangelo's vestibule, the Medici Chapel, the Chapel of the Princes, the Laurentian Library...the list goes on. Make sure to give yourself a good slug of time here.

THE BEST MARKETS

Florence's markets are part of its charm. Whether it is antiques, leather goods, fresh food or flowers, Florence has a market for it. Here are the best markets - all worthy of spending time in.

Flower Market

Held every Thursday morning under the porticos in the Piazza delle Repubblica, this traditional flower market is a sea of colours and smells. A wide variety of mainly seasonal blooms, with some more ornate arrangements and pot plants. Buying flowers in Florence makes you feel like a local!

- Via Pellicceria, (Piazza delle Repubblica)
- Every Thursday: 08:00 AM - 2.00 PM

Mercato Centrale

Florence's "new market" was purpose-built in 1874 after the old market had to be relocated. This extensive market is over two floors based on a design similar to Les Halles in Paris. The ground floor is full of butchers, delicatessen and artisan shops selling local meats and delicacies - well worth popping in for a look or maybe to buy some delicious *Finocchiona* (Fennel salami). Many restaurants buy their food here, and locals shop here regularly. Upstairs is far more contemporary. It is a giant food hall/food court with all manner of local and international cuisine. It is very buzzy, good value and worth having at least one meal here.

- Piazza del Mercato Centrale
- Open Every Day

The Ciompi Market

A monthly antique market, nestled into the Piazza dei Ciompi, where you can browse a wide range of bric-a-brac antiques, design objects and other collectables. Quirky and fun, there is always something tempting here.

- Piazza dei Ciompi
- Last Sunday of every month: 09:00 AM - 4.00 PM

Il Mercatale

A monthly market of local producers selling the very best of Tuscan delicacies from Olive Oil, Vin Santo, Chianti, Cantuccini, salamis, truffle-infused jams, and honey. It's held in the Piazza delle Repubblica, great for strolling through, but make regular stops to taste, chat and buy!

- Piazza delle Repubblica
- First Saturday of the month: 08:00 AM - 8.00 PM

Mercatino delle Pulci

This is an antique and vintage clothing market in Sant'Ambrogio and neighbours the food market. Come here for vintage clothing, old books, collectables, and antiques.

- Largo Pietro Annigoni
- Monday - Saturday: 08:00 AM - 7.30 PM

Cascine Market

A weekly market pops up every Tuesday morning in the large Cascine Park. A mass of sellers offers everything from shoes to household items and food. It's basic and sprawling - about 3kms alongside the Arno, but it is very much a functional local market.

- Viale Abramo Lincoln
- Every Tuesday: 07:00 AM - 2.00 PM

Mercato Del Porcellino (Mercato Novo)

This gets its name from the Brass Boar fountain outside the magnificent Loggia del Mercato Nuovo building, which was originally built in 1547. It is largely a leather market, but you can also buy T-shirts, scarves, clothing, and other trinkets.

- Address: Piazza del Mercato Nuovo
- Monday - Sunday: 09:00 AM - 6.30 PM

Santo Spirito Artisan Market

Every second Sunday of the month, the Piazza Santo Spirito is filled with artisan stalls, selling everything from homemade jewellery, jams, foodstuff, ceramics, and other artisan items. On the 3rd Sunday, it becomes just a food market. Either way, it's a great way to browse, relax and soak up Florentine culture, with plenty of opportunity for a coffee or a glass of wine along the way,

- Piazza Santo Spirito
- Every second and third Sunday of the month

Fiesole Vintage Market

On the hill perched above Florence is the small market town of Fiesole. It offers the most dramatic view of Florence rooftops and the Duomo and hosts a monthly flea market offering collectables, vintage clothing, antiques, bric-à-brac and other rare and interesting objects. The best way to get there is the number 7 bus that departs every 30 minutes from Piazza San Marco and takes about 20 minutes to get to Fiesole.

· Piazza Mino da Fiesole, Fiesole
· First Sunday of every month: 09:00 AM - 4.00 PM

Fortezza da Basso

In a fantastic setting amongst the outer courtyards of the 16th Century Fortezza da Basso, this antique market has antiques, bric-à-brac, oil paintings, old books and other collectables. Always popular with the locals, this is a bustling market that takes place on the third weekend of every month.

· Viale Strozzi
· Third weekend of every month: 09:00 AM - 7.30 PM

San Lorenzo

Originally situated in front of the Basilica San Lorenzo but now relocated nearer the Mercato Centrale, this is Florence's original Leather market. Every possible type of leather goods is found here - from beautiful jackets and shoes to leather-bound books and bookmarks. Other good-value "luxuries" such as jewellery, scarves, and ceramics have been added to the market. Most items are genuine and of suitable value but check for "Made in Italy" and ensure your valuables are safe. It is a crowded market full of tourists, and pickpockets abound here.

· Address: Piazza San Lorenzo
· Open every day.

Mercato di Sant'Ambrogio

This is one of Florence's best markets, mainly because very few tourists know about it. It is fabulous for fresh meat, amazing cheeses, fruits, and vegetables. But as it is predominantly a local market, there are also second-hand/vintage clothes and general household items.

- Address: Piazza Lorenzo Ghiberti
- Monday - Sunday: 07:00 AM - 1.00 PM

THE BEST MUSEUMS

Florence has an abundance of museums. From fashion (Salvatore Ferragamo Museum) to artisan leathercrafts, from sculpture to Cantucci biscuits. Many "traditional guidebooks" will cover these in greater detail and be invaluable companions as you delve into Florence's unique cultural heritage. So, in this book, I've just highlighted some obvious "must sees" that it would be unforgivable to visit Florence without at least ticking these off your list.

Palazzo Vecchio

Famously situated in the corner of the Piazza della Signoria and with its 94-metre-high tower (Torre'Danolfo), this is one of Florence's great centrepieces and still the city's administrative heart. The mayor has his office there even to this day. Most notable are the massive state room - built to house the 500 council members, the Medici apartments, and, of course, Michelangelo's Davide that stands outside the front. Movie buffs that watched Dan Brown's 'Inferno" might also recognise parts of it!

· Piazza della Signoria

Uffizi Gallery

This is the city's art museum - arguably the world's oldest public gallery. It's stuffed full of priceless works by Botticelli, Caravaggio, Giotto, Michelangelo, Raphael, and Titian, and there is way too much to see in one day. It is best viewed out of season when it is cooler and there are fewer tourists. It is Well worth doing a "skip the queue" booking for this one, but all tickets have specific times, so do plan.

· Piazzale degli Uffici, 6

Ponte Vecchio

Thankfully spared the bombing during World War 2, this famous Florentine landmark houses goldsmiths and jewellery designers in the small original workshops that hang over the edge of the bridge. One of the best-preserved mediaeval bridges in the world, it is impossible to visit Florence without crossing it, pausing on it or just admiring it.

- Ponte Vecchio

Il Grande Museo del Duomo

The Duomo is the landmark that defines Florence as it soars over the rooftops. An architectural and construction masterpiece by Brunelleschi in 1432 (work began 150 years before), has recently had its museum revamped and there are over 750 stunning works of art, over 3 floors. It shouldn't really be missed but do book - the crowds and queues can be long.

- Piazza del Duomo, 9

Palazzo Strozzi

Until well into the 20th century, this was the family home of the Strozzi family; it is now the contemporary art's "yang" to the city of Florence Renaissance art "ying". It is always full of fascinating contemporary exhibits and has a great cafe worth checking out on its own merits.

- Piazza degli Strozzi

Galleria Dell'Accademia

Its most famous exhibit is the original Michelangelo David, but there is also a fantastic collection of antique musical instruments, plaster casts by famous sculptures and some stunning art.

· Via Ricasoli 58-60

THE BEST NIGHT CLUBS

There are lots of new clubs popping up in Florence. Many are aimed at tourists and have a slightly seedy vibe about them. There are so many bars and great places in Florence where you can drink and listen to live music (many of which are covered in this book) that it is hard to determine what to include under Nightclubs. So I've picked a couple of popular places where you can find visiting bands or great DJs, and really dance. Have fun!

NDF

A small bar come nightclub with live music. There is a good selection of cocktails, but it is more of a sit, listen and drink place than get up and dance until dawn.

- Borgo San Frediano 13,

Tenax

It's one of the more established nightclubs. Large basement club with top quality DJs with an 18-30s crowd, many of whom are local Italians.

- Via Pratese 46

Manduca

Large club with inside and outside spaces, not far from the main train station, so nice and central and open mainly in Summer. Very much the place to go on a Saturday night.

- Via San Biagio a Petriolo 2/A

Viper Theatre

Many international bands that play Florence do so at the Viper Theatre. There is an excellent programme and incredible live music, and often a chance to hear a well-known band play a set in a more intimate place. When a live band is not playing, then there are DJs, and it becomes more of a classic Disco. Huge fun.

· Via Pistoiese

Rex Café

This is a lounge bar that transforms into a nightclub and is centrally located. Very much an art deco nautical theme, this is a stylish club with good seating and plenty of amazing cocktails. The music ranges from live jazz to DJs spinning vinyl. Quite hip and fun.

· Via Fiesolana, 25/R

THE BEST PARKS

Florence has many green spaces - some of which are more cultivated, famous and on the traditional tourist routes, whilst others are secret courtyards or gardens that are private. But of those that are publicly accessible, there are also some hidden gems. This is a short list of those worthy of a visit!

Boboli Gardens

The 11 acres of manicured parkland is what I always envisage when I think of Ordered Italian gardens. Created for the Medici family when they lived in the Pitti Palace, the gardens are beautiful, peaceful and worth a visit.

· Piazza Pitti, 1

Rose Gardens

Tourists do not often visit the Rose Gardens, but of course, they are more seasonal due to the nearly 400 rose species on show. Some modern sculptures break up the rose planting, but the scent is absolutely heavenly.

· Viale Giuseppe Poggi 2

Bardini Gardens

The secret to this garden is that there is also a small bar here. Not nearly as many people come here as the nearby and expansive Boboli, but it is still a beautifully manicured and typical Renaissance garden worthy of a visit, as it is far less crowded and free.

· Costa San Giorgio 2

Horticultural Gardens

These gardens are very much a summer venue and quite hip in their own way, as there is a bar and live music in the summer.

· Via Vittorio Emmenuele II 4

Cascine Park

The weekly market (see Cascine market) held here is one of the high-lights of this enormous park - the largest public space in Florence. It is popular with runners, families, lovers, and pensioners alike. There is also a public swimming pool here, which is very popular in the warmer months.

- Piazzale delle Cascine

4

THE BEST PLACES TO DRINK

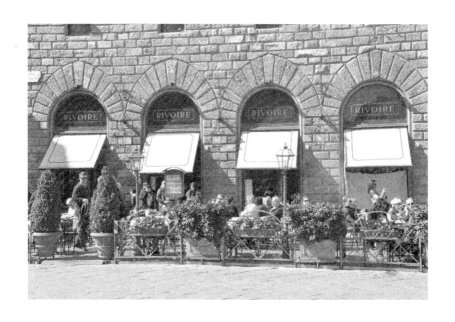

Florence is a place where things take the time they take. It is a place to sit and savour a drink - whether that is an *espresso, aperitivo* or *digestivo.* Cafes serving you your morning Cappuccino turn into restaurants at lunchtime and then morph into bars or nightclubs at night. Each has its style, ambience and clientele. It's very much a personal thing, but here are some proven and tested recommendations.

BEST CAFES

Rivoire

Right in the heart of the Piazza della Signoria this elegant old Florentine Cafe is in a prime location. Chic waiters serve perfect but expensive cappuccinos. It's definitely a place to be seen and to watch others. You will pay a premium for the location and if you sit down. Why not drink an espresso at the bar, which will be cheaper (though less easy to spot everyone!)? Arguably one of the best hot chocolates in Florence, too!

- Piazza della Signoria, 5/R
- Monday to Sunday: 07:30 AM - 11:00 PM

Caffè Concerto Paszkowski

I always have at least one coffee here every time I visit Florence. This is one of Florence's oldest and most unchanged cafes/bars. Right in the centre, it gets a great mixture of locals, businesses, and tourists. It is grand and important to Florence's history and literary tradition. It is officially a national monument and switches effortlessly from cafe to restaurant for lunch and then to bar. In the evenings, there is still live music. There is a good choice of food and vegetarian options, though you are paying the price for being in one of Florence's last great "institutions"

- Piazza delle Repubblica,
- Monday – Sunday: 08:00 AM – 01:00 AM

Ditta Artginale

There are now 3 locations of this excellent cafe, which manages to blend the best of local cafe (a cappuccino and croissant) with the more American style (space to work larger, more "international" drinks) and turns into a great bar in the evening. My favourite one is in Via dell Spello which is close to the Pitti Palace. It has plenty of space for those looking to work and drink coffee. Due to the large space, this has quite a student crowd. Coffees are reasonably priced, the WIFI is good, and there are excellent choices to eat; the avocado on toast is excellent. The one on Via de Neri Is a little too touristy for my liking, although the formula is very popular. The third is at Ponte di San Niccolo and is a little outside the tourist route (good!) but closer to the Piazzale Michelangelo.

- Via dei Neri, 32
- Via dello Sprone, 3/R
- Lungarno Benvenuto Cellini 3/R
- Monday–Friday: 07:30 AM – 10:30 PM
- Saturday to Sunday: 08:00 AM – 10:30 PM

Ben Caffé

For a cafe that is in the heart of the tourist area, Ben caffé (translates as "good coffee") is a bit of a hidden gem. It is seldom too busy and offers a wide range of different coffees, breakfast specials" and many other things to eat. Perfect for a cappuccino and a croissant and a few moments to catch your breath before plunging back into the crowded streets of the *Centro Storico.*

- Via delle Ocche, 7
- Monday to Sunday: 07:30 AM - 3:00 PM

La Ménagère

La Ménagère is a concept store that combines a restaurant, flower shop, home store and cafe under a single roof. Later in the day, it becomes more of a restaurant, but it is perfect for a coffee and pastry if you are up in this part of town in the morning. You'll find many people taking pictures for their Instagram accounts, but less so in the morning when it is quieter. In the evening, it becomes a bar and serves excellent (if expensive) cocktails, which is why it can sometimes get mixed reviews.

- Via de' Ginori, 8/R
- Monday to Sunday: 07:30 AM - 02:00 AM

Chiaroscuro

This is a truly authentic small Florentine Cafe. The proximity to the Duomo can make it busy, but the compact nature and the number of locals standing at the bar drinking a quick espresso hint at its old Florentine history and vibe. It's really good value, with great coffee served simply and at great prices. The pastries are pretty good too! If you have a sweet tooth, I am told that the hot chocolate is especially good.

- Via del Corso, 36/R
- Monday to Sunday: 07:00 AM - 09:30 PM

Caffe Mantra

Just a few minutes walk from the Basilica di Santa Croce, this great little cafe has amazing coffee and nice pastries but also a really good vibe. The owner is passionate about coffee, and you get a great mix between old Florentine purism and new-world enthusiasm. There is not much to look at from the outside, but the quality of the coffee speaks for itself. they also make ice-cream coffee specialties such as affogato (coffee with gelato), which is a real treat.

- Via dalla Mattonaia, 24/R
- Monday to Saturday: 08:00 AM - 4:00 PM

Melaleuca

Arguably the best craft coffee in Florence and with an international menu, this is an incredibly well-regarded small cafe by locals and visitors alike. It is also great for brunch and has some of the best pastries in Florence, but that is a hard claim to live up to, given the competition.

- Lungarno delle Grazie 18
- Monday to Saturday : 09:00 AM - 4:00 PM

simBIOsi

The BIO in the name hints at the organic focus of this cafe/restaurant. There are some amazing organic food options here, so it is perfect for a brunch or light lunch and a great place for a morning coffee. You can have a classic Italian coffee served alongside bistro-style food such as crepes, omelettes, charcuterie boards, sandwiches, and salads. Try to grab a seat at the window or bar to enjoy your coffee and pastry.

- Via de' Ginori, 64/R
- Monday to Sunday: 11:30 AM - 11:30 PM

Caffè Gilli

A traditional place for coffee with a great location and a good alternative to the Caffè Concerto Paszkowski. It's not the cheapest place for your morning cappuccino, but it's totally authentic. Also, some of the smartest restrooms in the centre of town!

- Via Roma, 1/R (Piazza della Repubblica).
- Monday to Sunday : 08:00 AM - 11:59 PM

Caffè Scudieri

Another traditional Florentine cafe/bar with a great location in the heart of the *Centro Storico* is always busy, and whilst it is not the cheapest place for a coffee, it is very much a classic. The pastries are good but a little limited compared to some other cafes.

- Piazza di San Giovanni 19/R
- Sunday to Thursday: 07:00 AM - 11:00 PM
- Friday to Saturday: 07:00 AM - 11:59 PM

Il Caffè del Verone

The Caffè del Verone is an excellent spot for brunch/lunch, but perhaps less ideal for that quick coffee on the go! It is located on a fantastic terrace within an ancient loggia, situated in the former drying room of the Ospedale degli Innocenti, so it has stunning views. It is a cafeteria-style restaurant, and the cafe is perfect for brunch or lunch. It is also fun for *aperitivo*. But I think there are other more atmospheric places for that time of day. The café is also accessible to those without a museum ticket.

- Piazza della Santissima Annunziata, 13
- Monday to Sunday: 10:00 AM – 8:00 PM

Le Murate Caffè Letterario

A great vibe to this place. Coffee is really good value, and although it is a little off the tourist track, the atmosphere and prices always mean it is popular. This is a great place to spend a while or to work. There is also live music, so do check out the schedule online. the *aperitivo* buffet starts at 7 pm and is popular with students because of its good value.

- Piazza delle Murate
- Monday to Friday: 08:00 AM – 01:00 AM
- Saturday to Sunday: 11:00 AM – 01:00 AM

La Cité

A local favourite because it combines a bookstore with a great cafe, this is a place to come and spend time. Find a place in a cosy corner or on one of the many comfy chairs and while away the hours. In the evening, this livens up to an event location for live music or book readings. If it looks full, try the less crowded upstairs or basement.

- Borgo S. Frediano, 20/R
- Monday to Sunday: 10:00 AM – 10:00 PM

Pasticceria Nencioni

There is tremendous value at this tiny local coffee spot. It is very much a "hole in the wall" café; there are only a couple of tables and a couple of places to stand. But it more than makes up for this with the quality of its coffee, pastries, and homemade desserts, which you can take with you (try their panna cotta!). Always packed with locals, I enjoy a cappuccino here as much as any other location in Florence.

- Via Pietrapiana, 24/R
- Monday to Saturday: 07:30 AM – 8:00 PM
- Sunday: 07:30 AM – 7:00 PM

Pop Cafe

Perhaps the simplest of cafe's and yet one that just imbues everything I love about Florence. Set in the Piazza Santo Spirito, this tiny almost scruffy cafe serves amazing coffee, and delicious simple pastries and is beloved by locals, who will invite you to share their table and chat away to you as if you belonged. Heaven.

- Piazza Santo Spirito, 18/R
- Monday to Sunday: 08:00 AM – 02:00 AM

BEST APERITIVO BARS

A drink at the end of the working day, with friends or colleagues, is part of Italian life, and Florence is no exception. Watch the sun go down, sip a glass of Prosecco and munch on some delicious Tuscan snacks. *Aperitivo* time is just the most beautiful part of the day.

Tamerò

Quirky and edgy, this is a pasta bar with a difference. A converted workshop with graffiti-covered walls, you can grab a classic Spritz and a buffet of pasta from 6.30 pm.

- Piazza Santo Spirito 11/R

Sabor Cubano

Cuba comes to Italy. This tiny bar very close to the Mercato Centrale not surprisingly specialises in Cuban rum-based cocktails. Some more inventive ideas challenge some classics on the menu. Hip and always busy!

- Via Sant'Antonino 64

Ambiè

A hidden gem, as it is right next to the Ponte Vecchio, but set in a quiet courtyard. It's a quirky bric-à-brac shop and wine bar where vintage furniture meets modern cocktails. With an eclectic cocktail menu, some delicious and inventive nibbles, and an opportunity to shop while you drink! Nothing matches - intentionally - and cocktails are served in antique glasses from all over Europe. This is one of those places that most guidebooks miss.

- Piazzetta dei Del Bene 7a
- Tuesday to Saturday: 10:00 AM - 10:00 PM
- Sunday: 12:00 PM - 10:00 PM

Sei Divino

A great selection of over 200 wines, this wine bar is only about 350m from the Ponte Vecchio yet is cosy and has a good atmosphere. Great cheese, cold meats, and salamis to accompany some great wines.

- Borgo Ognissanti 42/R

Fusion Bar in Gallery Hotel Art

Just next to the Ponte Vecchio on the northern side is a small courtyard, and this hip, quirky hotel is packed full of Art. It has a Fusion Bar that serves a great range of traditional cocktails, some with a local twist, others as variations on an international theme.

 · Vicolo dell'Oro 5

Le Volpi e l'Uva

Easily missed, but a delightful wine bar full (not difficult, it is small!) with locals and serving wine by the glass. They specialise in small-volume Italian wines, and the list is extensive and delicious. Not surprisingly, the locals love this place. Great food, especially their Tagliere plate of local cheeses and meats.

 · Piazza dei Rossi 18

La Casa Del Vino

A truly "local" wine bar that is standing room only that goes back nearly 150 years and is just around the corner from the Mercato Centrale. There is a great selection of wines by the glass, awesome crostini, and sandwiches.

 · Via Dell'Ariento 16

Il Santino

A tiny haunt frequented mainly by locals that specialises in local Tuscan wines. The simple but delicious food served in tapas style helped to put this "hole in the wall" on the map. But it is small... so small that a family would pack the place out.

- Via di santo Spirito, 60

THE BEST ROOFTOP BARS

THE BEST PLACES TO DRINK

Most of the rooftop bars are part of hotels. They are small and relatively exclusive, and most demand a smart casual dress code. Nearly all of them have amazing views, a comprehensive wine and cocktail menu, and the opportunity to have snacks and nibbles. Some you pay for the privilege of being there either in the price of the drink or a minimum spend. Others charge for the drinks but then provide free food. Either way, an *aperitivo* on a rooftop in Florence as the sun goes down over the Arno is a magical way to spend the evening.

Rooftop bar at La Rinascente

Tucked away on the top of the Rinascente Department store in Piazza delle Repubblica is this cosy rooftop bar. Come here for the rooftop views of the Duomo and come early as it is small, and by the time the sun sets, there is a queue to get in!

- Piazza delle Repubblica 4

La Terrazza Del Minerva at the Hotel Grande Minerva

This rooftop bar at the Minerva Hotel has a 360-degree view of the city. It offers a comprehensive cocktail list and some good snacks, but it is quite expensive compared to other bars. It is seasonal - usually opening in April and closing by the end of October.

- Piazza Santa Maria Novella, 16

La Terrazza at the Hotel Continentale

This vies with SES-TO at the Westin Hotel for great views over the Arno. Set atop the Hotel Continental, it is a stylish bar but comes with a hefty minimum spend if you are not a hotel guest.

· Lungarno degli Acciaiuoli, 2/r

Loggia Rooftop Bar at the Hotel Palazzo Guadagni

Set in the Santo Spirito district, this loggia on top of the hotel provides a beautiful, exclusive feel yet remains unpretentious. It feels like you are visiting your wealthy Italian friends for the evening, albeit the decor in the Loggia has a slightly Moroccan feel with old lanterns, rattan chairs and lots of plants. Wine or prosecco is the order of the day here, although cocktails are also on offer. Some good nibbles, too!

· Piazza Santo Spirito, 9

Angel bar at the Hotel Calimala

This is a dangerous bar for all the right reasons. Stylish, low-key, relaxing, and an amazing 360 panorama, including the Duomo, it is also not that well known. It has a great wine list, fabulous cocktails, and lots to eat. It is the sort of place you go for a quick "sharpener" and leave hours later having had a fabulous evening.

B-Roof at the Hotel Baglioni

This is one of the city's more exclusive and stylish rooftop bars. It does have the most stunning location and, hence, a view of the Duomo, but it is pretty pricey. It is elegant and popular so you will need a reservation. The rooftop bar is only open in the summer months, but there is also a good restaurant up there, too. From Wednesdays to Saturdays, the *aperitivo* is accompanied by live music.

- Piazza dell'Unita Italiana, 6

Divina Terrazza at the Hotel Grand Cavour

The saving grace of this rooftop bar is the view of the Duomo. The cocktails and snacks are okay – nothing spectacular and reasonably priced. The ambiance and decor is about average, but the view is definitely worth the trip up to the bar and arguably the price of a cocktail!

- Via del Proconsolo, 3

SE-STO Bar at the Westin

Few rooftop bars can match the view over the river Arno. The rooftop bar at the Westin offers great cocktails from 7 pm. Not the cheapest, but the free buffet of nibbles and eats that accompanies it means that, timed right, there is no need for supper!

- Piazza Ognissanto 3

THE BEST WINE BARS

As I mentioned before, some of the cafes are really bars, and so you can get a great glass of wine in many of these places. But there are also dedicated wine bars with more extensive wine lists or only serve wine.

Amblè

A hidden gem, as it is right next to the Ponte Vecchio, but set in a quiet courtyard. It's a quirky bric-a-brac shop and Wine bar where vintage furniture meets modern cocktails. With an eclectic cocktail menu, some delicious and inventive nibbles, and an opportunity to shop while you drink! Nothing matches - intentionally - and cocktails are served in antique glasses from all over Europe; this is one of those places that most guidebooks miss.

- Piazzetta dei Del Bene 7a
- Tuesday to Saturday: 10:00 AM - 10:00 PM
- Sunday: 12:00 PM - 10:00 PM

Caffè Gilli

A traditional place for coffee with a great location and a really good alternative to the Caffè Concerto Paszkowski. It's not the cheapest place for your morning cappuccino, but it's totally authentic. Also, some of the smartest restrooms in the centre of town!

- Via Roma, 1/R (Piazza della Repubblica).
- Monday to Sunday: 08:00 AM - 11:59 PM

Procacci

As somebody allergic to truffles, sadly, this is not a place I can spend time in. But for those who are not allergic - and I suspect that is all of you - this is a truffle haven and has been since 1885. It's a great bar with an elegant vibe, and a glass of Prosecco or wine perfectly accompanies the small eats, many of which have truffles in them.

- Via de' Tornabuoni 64/R
- Monday to Saturday: 10:00 AM - 9:00 PM
- Sunday 11:00 AM - 8:00PM

Sei Divino

You can tell that this shop/bar is run by a sommelier as there are hundreds of wines to buy and taste. Served with a daily changing menu of delicious local snacks that show off the local Tuscan gourmet food to its best.

- Borgo Ognissanti 42/R.
- Wednesday to Monday: 6:00 PM – 01:00 AM

Le Murate Caffè Letterario

A great vibe to this place. Coffee is really good value, and although it is a little off the tourist track, the atmosphere and prices always mean it is popular. This is a great place to spend a while or to work. There is also live music, so do check out the schedule online. The *aperitivo* buffet starts at 7 pm and is popular with students because of its good value.

- Piazza delle Murate (Sant'Ambrogio)
- Monday to Friday: 08:00 AM – 01:00 AM
- Saturday to Sunday: 11:00 AM – 01:00 AM

Ditta Artigninale

There are now 3 locations of this excellent cafe, which manages to blend the best of local cafe (a cappuccino and croissant) with the more American style (space to work larger, more "international" drinks) and turns into a great bar in the evening. My favourite one is in Via dell Spello which is close to the Pitti Palace. It has plenty of space for those looking to work and drink coffee. Due to the large space, this has quite a student crowd. Coffees are reasonably priced, the WIFI is good, and there are excellent choices to eat; the avocado on toast is excellent. The one on Via de Neri Is a little too touristy for my liking, although the formula is the same and it is very popular. The third is at Ponte di San Niccolo and is a little outside the tourist route (good!) but closer to the Piazzale Michelangelo. In the evening, the cocktails begin, and with over 50 gins on offer, many are gin-based.

- Via dei Neri, 32
- Via dello Sprone, 3/R
- Lungarno Benvenuto Cellini 3/R
- Monday-Friday: 07:30 AM - 10:30 PM
- Saturday to Sunday: 08:00 AM - 10:30 PM

Cafe 1926

This eclectic, almost Parisian-themed cafe and bar has a lot of charm. Part gentleman's club, Parisian Cafe and art deco museum, the cocktails are amazing, and with nearly 400 bottles on offer, you are spoilt for choice.

- Via Giovanni Battista Niccolini 30/R
- Monday to Friday: 07:00 AM - 01:00 AM
- Saturday: 08:00 AM - 01:00 AM

Rasputin

Originally known only by the locals and word of mouth, this feels like Tsarist Russia has come to Florence. The cocktail barmen really know their art, and there are hundreds of different bottles from which their mixology skills are tested. It still doesn't advertise or have a street number, so you must ring to get the directions. But it's worth it!

- Borgo Tegolaio
- Sunday to Thursday: 08:00 PM - 02:00 AM
- Friday to Saturday : 21:00 PM - 03:00 AM

Il Santino

A tiny haunt frequented mainly by locals that specialises in local Tuscan wines. The simple but delicious food served in tapas style helped to put this "hole in the wall" on the map. But it is small... so small that a family would pack the place out.

- Via di santo Spirito, 60
- Monday to Sunday: 12:30 PM - 11:00 PM

Pint of view

Never let it be said that everything in Florence is about Tuscan food and wine. Pint of view offers artisan and craft beers, as well as artisan cocktails. These are then paired by Korean/Tuscan fusion food under a Korean chef. Quirky yet delicious.

- Borgo Tegolaio, 17/R
- Monday to Wednesday: 06:00 PM - 11:59 PM
- Thursday to Saturday: 6:00 PM - 02:00 AM
- Sunday: 12:00 PM - 23:59 PM

Le Volpi e L'Uva

Easily missed, but a delightful wine bar full (Not difficult, it is small!) with locals and serving wine by the glass. They specialise in small-volume Italian wines; the list is extensive and delicious. Not surprisingly, the locals love this place. Great food, especially their Tagliere plate of local cheeses and meats.

- Piazza dei Rossi 18
- Monday to Saturday: 11:00 AM – 09:00 PM

Mad Souls and Spirits

Genuinely inventive and quirky mixology at its best. There is not much more to say other than to go there and try some of their signature cocktails! Or a glass of wine!

- Borgo San Frediano 36-38/R

5

THE BEST PLACES TO EAT

THE BEST RESTAURANTS AND TRATTORIA

I 'm always hesitant to recommend restaurants to people because so much depends on what you like, what mood you are in, what the occasion is, the chef, and what ingredients were sourced that day. It is hard to eat poorly in Florence, so to be honest, almost anywhere is worth a try. But here is a small, curated selection of some of my favourites over the years. They range in style, cost, atmosphere, and menu!

Trattoria Sostanza

For over 150 years, this unpretentious trattoria has earned its place as a Florentine favourite. The food is simple - based on the hearty regional "peasant food". Their Bistecca Fiorentina - the local T-Bone speciality - is worthy of note, and some of their lighter dishes are memorable too. There are only about 6 tables, so you do need to book.

- Via del Porcellana 25/R
- Monday–Saturday: 12:30 PM - 2:00 PM and 7:30 PM - 9:45 PM

Trattoria L'Ortone

A simple Tuscan trattoria is in vogue with the locals and the Michelin guide (though not for its price, which is still very reasonable!). The dishes are mainly regional and always seasonal. Both the food and the wine are worthy of note and not overly expensive.

- Piazza Lorenzo Ghiberti, 87/R
- Monday–Sunday: 12:15 PM - 2:30 PM and 7:00 PM - 10:30 PM

Cantinetti Antinori

One of Florence's oldest families, which has been producing wine locally since 1385, has opened this restaurant on the ground floor of their family palazzo. The ingredients are fresh and produced on the Antinori extensive estates, and the quality of them speaks for itself. This is a sophisticated and stylish restaurant frequented by a wealthy and highbrow local crowd, but one that also welcomes anyone with a discerning eye for quality food and great wine.

- Piazza degli Antinori, 3
- Monday-Saturday: 12:30 PM - 2:30 PM and 7:00 PM - 10:30 PM

Braciere Malatesta

Bistecca Fiorentina is almost a religion in Florence. It is a particular "on the bone" cut that is substantial but still requires real skill to cook to perfection. And this is where Braciere Malatesta has built its reputation. The Baglioni family has been serving both tourists and locals since 1954, but despite the more contemporary decor that has been recently implemented, the restaurant ethos and capabilities remain unchanged. Put simply, order the steak!

- Via Nazionale, 36/R
- Monday-Sunday: 12:00 PM - 3:00 PM and 7:00 PM - 11:00 PM

Arà: è SUD

A great fusion of balanced flavours with unique ingredients brings some Sicilian gourmet cooking to Florence. The dishes are well presented, of amazing value, and provide a welcome alternative to some of the heavier local Tuscan cuisine.

- Via della Vigna Vecchia, 4/R
- Wednesday to Monday: 02:00 PM - 11:00 PM

Gurdulù

At this Santo Spirito restaurant and cocktail bar, an unusual mix of Tuscan, Spanish and Balkan flavours is on offer. Ingredients are largely local, and it is no surprise that it is popular with locals and tourists. The decor is chic and upbeat and has an international feel, largely due to the bright blue walls, bronze lamps and antique film posters. It's sophisticated and yet also quite romantic.

- Via delle Caldaie 12
- Tuesday- Sunday: 7:30 PM - 11:00 PM

Osteria dell'Enoteca

Sophisticated yet modern, this restaurant in a vaulted ceiling wine cellar on the south side of the Arno works whether you are on a romantic evening, out with friends or even there on business. Not the largest of restaurants, so you will need to reserve. The dress code seems to be smart casual/elegant, and that's only fair since the food and wine certainly meet that brief.

- Via Romana 70/R
- Wednesday-Monday: 12:00 PM - 2:30 PM and 07:00 PM-10:30 PM

L'OV

The OV stands for Osteria Vegetariana or vegetarian hostelry, so it should come as no surprise that the menu is vegetarian. Many of the dishes are vegan and/or gluten-free. The menu is inventive, tasty, well-balanced, and supported by a good wine list, some of which are organic. Always popular, you will need to book.

- Piazza del Carmine 4/R
- Monday-Saturday 07:00 PM - 11:00 PM
- Sunday 12:00 PM - 03:00 PM

Zeb

This restaurant is getting rave reviews as far afield as Los Angeles and London. Zeb stands for Zuppa e Bollito - simple Tuscan soups and stews. But the cooking, whilst unpretentious, is superb. Amazing ingredients and inventive flavours, all perfectly balanced. Possibly fast becoming one of my favourite restaurants in Florence. The counter-style seating means you see everything, though it is small, so you must book.

- Via San Miniato 2/R
- Thursday to Tuesday: 12:00 PM - 3:30 PM and 7:30 PM - 10:30 PM

Trattoria Marione

This traditional trattoria wins on the quality of its traditional cooking. Famous throughout Florence for its Ragù di Cinghiale or Wild Boar sauce, it is hard to get a place at lunchtime because it is packed with locals. The best advice is to eat the seasonal specials or ask the waiter for their advice. It is fresh, local, and almost the definition of authentic Tuscan cuisine.

You will need to book though.

- Via della Spada, 27/R
- Monday to Sunday: 12:00 PM - 3:00 PM and 6:30 PM - 11:00 PM

I Giova

This is a family-run restaurant that has built a word-of-mouth reputation with locals. You might be the only tourists there, but don't worry; the owners are incredibly friendly. The decor is unusual, and the owners make the most of the available space, so the tables are packed together, but that's perfect for feeling embedded in the local way of life. The food is entirely local - the ingredients are bought daily from the local market, so the menu is forever changing.

- Borgo la Croce, 73/R
- Monday to Saturday: 12:00 PM - 3:00 PM and 7:30 PM - 11:00 PM

Osteria Santo Spirito

Often overlooked due to its position in the far corner of the Piazza Santo Spirito, this superb Osteria serves uncomplicated local food. The portions are generous, and this is a place for a long-relaxed dinner. Do try their Gnocchi - they are famous for them. You may need to book as this is popular and gets good ratings on the leading travel sites.

- Piazza Santo Spirito, 16/R
- Monday to Saturday: 12:00 PM - 3:00 PM and 7:30 PM - 11:00 PM

Golden View

The name does not disappoint. This restaurant is perched on a balcony over the Arno, with an uninterrupted view of the Ponte Vecchio. The view is, simply put, Golden. The menu ranges from local crostini to Oysters, and anything on the menu, paired with a chilled glass of wine, seems to make the view even more special.

- Via de' Bardi, 58/R
- Wednesday to Sunday: 12:00 PM - 3:00 PM and 6:30 PM - 11:00 PM

La Giostra

This is an exclusive yet romantic restaurant that is used to hosting royalty. Well, if truth be told, the restaurant is owned by the former Austrian royal family! It is a place of candelabra, decanters filled with gorgeous wine and carefully concocted Italian plates that are more gourmet than local. Hugely popular, reservations are a must.

- Borgo Pinti, 10-18/R
- Wednesday to Sunday: 12:30 PM - 2:30 PM and 7:00 PM - 01:00 AM

Cantina Barbagianni

Beloved by locals and only a stone's throw from La Giostra, Cantina Barbagianni is an unfussy restaurant with a loyal following. It focuses on Tuscan cuisine and does not disappoint with the quality of its food. It deserves to be more celebrated.

- · Via Sant'Egidio, 13/R
- · Wednesday to Sunday: 6:30 PM - 10:00 PM

THE BEST GELATO

For me, ice cream, or Gelato, is synonymous with Italy and Florence in particular. Legend has it that it was first created in Florence by Bernardo Buontalenti in the Sixteenth century. I remember the first time I came and saw the mounds of gelato with such vibrant and different colours; I was torn about whether to have a cone or a cup, let alone how many flavours. Most of the Gelateria offers a mix of ice creams (typically made with milk and without eggs in Italy) or sorbets. The flavours will vary from the traditional ones that all will stock to more adventurous ones, such as a zesty mojito. Rather than list each of the variances, my strong suggestion is just to go, look and try!!

Perché No!...

Literally translated as "Why not", this historical and tiny gelateria has been a part of the Florentine culture since 1939. Located in the prime position between the Piazza delle Repubblica and the Piazza della Signoria, it still has a loyal following from locals and tourists alike. They have traditional ice creams, sorbets and flavours but also offer some vegan-friendly options.

· Via Dei Tavolini 19/R, 50122, Florence Italy

My Sugar

This opened recently - in 2015 - and has quickly become popular amongst the locals. Just around the corner from the Mercato Centrale, the gelato is made fresh daily, and the owners are known for their seasonal flavours. They concentrate on 16 flavours and buy many of their ingredients from the local markets. This is really good artisan ice cream.

· Via de' Ginori 49/R

Carabè

Have you stood before Michelangelo's David and mused, "I could just do with an ice cream about now?" Thankfully, Carabè can tend to that desire and probably a few more. Known for their sensational Sicilian flavours, and their "granita", this shop is worth returning to many times. Oh, and if you like cannoli, then they fill them fresh on the spot here. They need a gym nearby, I fear too!

· Via Ricasoli, 60/R

Gelateria Vivaldi

This is a dangerous shop to go to…. not only is their ice cream fantastic, but their hot chocolate is also excellent. Worse still, they have comfy seats out the back, so you can really indulge and relax. You can also watch the ice cream being made in their kitchen, which is really fun.

· Via de' Renai, 15/R

Gelateria Della Passera

Don't let the tiny size of the kitchen fool you. This ice cream is made fresh daily and has both traditional and more adventurous flavours. They make ice cream and sorbets and are just off the main beaten track of Santo Spirito in the smaller Piazza della Passera.

· Via Toscanella, 15

Cantina del Gelato

Just alongside the Arno is this small "Cantina" or Cellar selling natural, artisan ice cream. So much better than most of the other overpriced, tourist traps ice cream shops in the immediate area, they have some really adventurous new flavours, including one of my favourites - Vin Santo and Cantuccini (one of my all-time favourite fusions of flavours but admittedly I am used to dunking the Cantuccini in the Vin Santo).

· Via de' Bardi, 31

Geltaria dei Neri

In the Sant Croce area, this great gelateria serves a mixture of traditional and unique ice creams and sorbets.

· Via dei Neri, 9-11/R

Gelatera Edoardo

Conveniently located opposite the Duomo, you can either enjoy one while you queue or reward yourself with one after you have climbed to the top of the tower. This gelateria produces its own waffle cones, and the ice cream is all organic.

· Piazza del Duomo, 45/R

Gelateria Santa Trinita

This is a popular gelateria with tourists and locals alike. It is just beside the Santa Trinita bridge, alongside the Arno in Santo Spirito.

- Piazza Frescobaldi 11-12/R

Antica Gelateria Fiorentina

Just around the corner from the Mercato Centrale and the San Lorenzo markets is this tiny hole-in-the-wall Gelateria. It offers fairly traditional flavours and some sorbets, but the quality is excellent.

- Via Faenza, 2a

6

THE BEST PLACES TO STAY

I t is easy to jump on one of the major hotel sites or AirbNb and find a myriad of different choices and at very different price points in Florence. With its amazing architecture, many of the hotels have a stated grandeur about them. More recently, smaller, more boutique offers have popped up in some of these converted palaces, convents, or old buildings. If you are after hostels (not covered in this book), there are at least 30 in Florence that a simple web search will uncover. To help you find the right place, here are a number I have either stayed in personally or have been vouched for and recommended by friends and locals I trust.

BEST HOTELS

Hotel Lungarno

As its name suggests, it is along the Arno, on the south side and just down from the Ponte Vecchio. It is a stylish hotel with a great lounge and wicked Negronis and has one of the best terraces and views of the nearby Ponte Vecchio. There is also an underground car park right next door, which is a rare find and very convenient if you have driven into Florence.

- Borgo S. Jacopo, 14

Gallery Hotel Art

Across the Arno is the sister hotel to the Hotel Lungarno. This stylish Art hotel, with amazing contemporary art exhibitions, oozes design yet still maintains the same exemplary levels of service, luxury, and indulgence of its more traditional sister.

- Vicolo dell'Oro 5

Ottantotto Firenze

A boutique hotel of 7 stylish rooms in a converted Palazzo, this hotel oozes romance and charm. There is no restaurant, but the breakfast will make you smile. A wonderful mix of bare walls, stylish furniture, crisp linen sheets, and a wonderful staff make this a little hidden gem.

- Via dei Serragli 88

SoprArno Suites

This is a great example of the gentrification of Santo Spirito, as this stylish hotel - 13 themed suites - was converted from the old newspaper building of La Repubblica. Charming, quiet, and understated, if Santo Spirito is your neighbourhood of choice, this should be on your list of places to stay.

- Via Maggio 35

Continentale

If you are over "Renaissancehen the Hotel Continentale could be the answer. It seems to almost sit on top of the Ponte Vecchio. The receptionists look like they are dressed in Gucci (they probably are), the European films running on a loop provide a designer feel, and the rooms are just well-understated luxury. The sky lounge is also an amazing place to watch the sunset over the Arno, drink in hand.

- Vicolo dell'Oro 6/R

Casa Howard

Centrally located within easy reach of the bustling Main train station at Santa Maria Novella, Casa Howard is set in an old palazzo with a private courtyard, providing a much-needed antidote to the frenetic pace of the *Centro Storico*. It's really a boutique B&B - there is no restaurant - but the focus has been on luxurious bedding and impeccable design so that it's difficult not to find it romantic or to make you feel indulged and special.

- Via della Scala, 18

Milu

If the retro feel is more to your taste, then look no further than Milu. It is a mid-sized boutique hotel and gallery, where the gallery extends into the hotel, up the stairs, and into your room! There is also a small terrace for hotel guests with a great view of the city skyline.

- Via Tornabuoni 8

7

THE BEST HAND-PICKED ACTIVITIES

A simple web search will uncover a myriad of different courses and activities. Whilst some, like "Mama Cooking", have their own web presence, the majority are best accessed through the excellent site www.viator.com, which helps to aggregate the smaller and more individual activities to make it easy for you to book. Most of the ones I have highlighted below can be booked through this site, but of course, there are some that I have discovered or suggested that are direct booking. For many of the museums and the cathedral, not only do you need to book tickets, but you can also join "Skip the Queue" groups, where for a small premium, you do not have to queue. Well worth it!

BEST WALKING TOURS

Take a walking tour through Florence and see some of the highlights of this renaissance city. Tours have all sorts of different focuses. Some that are worthy of mention are:

The Medici's and the Renaissance

Learn all about the famous family that shaped Florence.
https://www.viator.com/en-GB/tours/Florence

The Dark Side of Florence - Mysteries and Legends.

Hear about the curiosities, the intrigue, the betrayal and the murders
that are associated with some of the most beautiful landmarks in the
city.
https://www.viator.com/en-GB/tours/Florence

Florence Sunset Walking Tour with Wine & Food Tasting

Walk the city and discover Florence's "Wine Windows" and centuries-
old wine cellars. You'll taste amazing artisan cheese, learn to make a
negroni and even learn how to spot fake Gelato
https://www.viator.com/en-GB/tours/Florence

Discover the Art and History of Santa Croce Basilica

Whilst the official guide will really only show you or highlight the key
things I have mentioned in the section under Best Churches, the first
time you visit the Basilica, it can be a bit overwhelming, and this curated
tour helps you not to miss some of Florence's artistic highlights.
https://www.viator.com/en-GB/tours/Florence

Artisan Workshops: Private Walking Tour

These amazing tours can be tailored to your area of interest e.g. Wood carving, jewellery or leather or a mix of different workshops. One of the most fascinating behind-the-scenes activities.

https://www.artviva.com

Learn Italian as you Walk.

If you only have a day and want to combine a walking tour with some language learning, then Artviva's excellent and fun tour might meet your needs. It's about 2-3 hours long.

https://www.artviva.com

Amazing Women in Florence – A Walking Tour.

A 3-hour walk through Florence learning about the women from the Dark Ages to the Baroque that helped to shape Florence.

https://www.artviva.com

A Gentleman's Tour – Shop, Style & Taste in Italy

Another of Artiva's excellent tours, this time for men that includes a visit to a bespoke tailor, shoemaker, barber, wine cellar and much more

https://www.artviva.com/

THE BEST LANGUAGE CLASSES

When I first came to Florence, I studied at the Istituto Europeo, and I still rate it as one of the best language schools in the city. There are many ways to study Italian, and of course, it really takes time, so visiting for a weekend is unlikely to provide enough opportunity to progress your language skills. However, if you have a week or more, you can take individual lessons or join a group - which is better value. Courses run from a single week to months or years depending on the level. The best language schools are:

Istituto Europeo

- Via del Parione n. 1 (Tornabuoni), 50123 Firenze,
- E-mail: info@istitutoeuropeo.it
- Tel: +39 055 238 1071
- www.istitutoeuropeo.org

Parola

- Borgo Santa Croce, 17 – 50122 Firenze
- +39 055 242182 +39 328 8997420
- info@parola.it
- www.parola.it

Istituto Il David

- Via de Vecchietti, 1 - 50123 Florence
- +39 055 21 61 10
- info@davidschool.com
- https://www.davidschool.com/en/

British Institute

- Language Centre
- Viale Mazzini 10
- 50132 Firenze
- Tel: +39 055 2677 81
- Email: info@britishinstitute.it

THE BEST ART CLASSES

Paint & Wine

One of the many courses run by the Florence Art Studio. They also do a master's, portraits and other courses from days to months. But this is a fun and flexible course and combines great mediums: Art and wine. You can do evening private groups, so the best thing is to head to their website:

https://www.theflorenceartstudio.com/paintdraw-and-wine

5 Mornings Still Life Painting Guided Workshop in Florence

5-morning sessions with professional artists that take you through, step-by-step - the creation of your own still life.
https://www.viator.com/en-GB/tours/Florence

5 mornings guided Clay Class at The Florence Studio

An intense 5-day workshop where you learn to sculpt in clay, supported by a professional sculptor. You can choose to create an original work or copy an existing piece and take it home with you at the end.
https://www.viator.com/en-GB/tours/Florence

Oil Painting Class in Florence

A 3-hour workshop that introduces you to *ChiaroScuro*, colours, flesh tones and different types of "edges".
https://www.viator.com/en-GB/tours/Florence

Drawing and Watercolour Workshop in the Heart of Florence

It is a chance to either start to sketch or perhaps dust off some old skills and get reacquainted with drawing and watercolour, guided by a local artist and using the backdrop of Florence's magnificent architecture, streets and views to create endless opportunities.
https://www.viator.com/en-GB/tours/Florence

THE BEST PHOTOGRAPHY COURSES

Florence Private Photography Workshop

A guided photo workshop, where under the watchful eye of an award-winning photographer, you will perfect your style, take stunning and unusual images of Florence and have a chance to practise new techniques.

https://www.viator.com/en-GB/tours/Florence

Night Photo Walking tour

A 3-hour evening photo walk with a professional photographer that helps you improve low light techniques and capture some amazing iconic images of Florence at dusk and at night.

https://www.viator.com/en-GB/tours/Florence

Private Photoshoot

A 90-minute professional photoshoot with Florence as a backdrop. The 20 best images are then made available to you for your use!

https://www.viator.com/en-GB/tours/Florence

THE BEST COOKING AND WINE COURSES

Mama Florence Cooking Classes

There are almost too many of these to mention, but I think the various courses run by Mama Florence are without equal. Their prices vary depending on whether it is a private course, individual or group, but the sorts of classes available are.

- Pizza and Gelato
- Gelato and Biscotti
- Market tour and pasta-making
- Pasta Carbonara making
- Gluten-free pasta
- Market tour and Tuscan cooking class

https://www.mamaflorence.com/

Florentine Steak Cooking Class

Unique to Florence is the Bistecca Fiorentina. It's a massive slab of beef on the bone and is notoriously difficult to cook well. Attend this masterclass, learn all of the secrets and eat what you cook!

https://www.artviva.com/

Vegan and Vegetarian classes

Alternatively, Artvia run some excellent Vegan cooking classes.

https://www.artviva.com/

THE BEST PERFUME-MAKING COURSES

Make your own Perfume.

Work with a master perfumer and learn how he makes different fragrances. He will help you to select your own ingredients to make your own perfume which you can then leave with a bottle of it.

https://www.viator.com/en-GB/tours/Florence/

THE BEST JEWELLERY MAKING COURSES

Create and forge your piece of Jewellery.

Escape the bustle of Florence for a day and spend it instead with a master craftsman in his workshop and make your own piece of silver jewellery.

https://www.viator.com/en-GB/tours/Florence/

THE BEST POTTERY MAKING COURSES

How to make handmade Tuscan Pottery

Spend a day with a master potter in his family-run workshop and learn how to work raw clay, fire, and glaze your own work, which, once it is cooled and hardened, can then be shipped to your home destination.

https://www.viator.com/en-GB/tours/Florence/

BEST DAY TRIPS

Tuscany by Bike: Full-day Tuscany Bike Tour

It's a great way to see some of the countryside outside of Florence. This is a full-day bike tour through the Tuscan countryside and olive groves and manages to fit in lunch, wine tasting and a vineyard tour.

https://www.artviva.com/product/tuscany-bike-one-day-tour/

Florentine Hills on an electric vespa

This fun tour includes wine, food, and coffee tastings in the Mugello and Fiesole hills around Florence. It is huge fun and very much an Italian experience.

https://www.viator.com/en-GB/tours/Florence/

Self-Drive Vintage Fiat 500 Tour

Why not really turn back the years and hire a classic Fiat Cinquecento and explore the Tuscan hills? Options include either a visit to a vineyard or to taste various delicious Tuscan foods. Either way, you can live *"La Dolce Vita"* for a few hours.

https://www.viator.com/en-GB/tours/Florence/

8

CONCLUSION

I hope you find some or many of these "insider" tips helpful in allowing you to glimpse a little bit more under the skin of the Florence I love, and I hope it means that you will have an appetite to come back to this fantastic city and explore more of her secrets.

It's been an almost cathartic process to finally put some of this down in a single document. I will endeavour to produce a second edition with newer images, updated places and more tips.

If you can make the time, I would really appreciate you leaving a review on Amazon. It helps to have honest feedback, and the more reviews (and hopefully high-scoring ones), the better the results in the algorithm, which will mean more people will see and benefit from the tips in the book. It takes only a minute or two, and I would be hugely appreciative.

Many thanks

Marco

Firenze, January 2024.

9

RESOURCES

ppetite, C. |. C. (2022, May 27). Ara e' Sud: *Is this New Sicilian?* - Curious Appetite. Curious Appetite. https://thecuriousappetite.com/2016/05/25/ara-e-sud-sicilian-food-florence/

ArtViva. (2023a, August 11). *Italy's best Tours - Private Florence Tours.* https://www.artviva.com/destinations/florence-tours/

ArtViva. (2023b, November 9). *High quality tours & experiences in Italy - ArtViva.* https://www.artviva.com/

Best Florence Cooking Classes | Mama Florence. (n.d.). MamaFlorence. https://www.mamaflorence.com/

EXPERT TIPS BY: Alexa Schnee Florence Local Expert. (n.d.). *Florence Nightlife: Viper Theater.* 10Best. https://10best.usatoday.com/destinations/italy/florence/florence/nightlife/viper-theater/

Florence Neighborhoods - complete guide! | Florencewise. (n.d.). Florencewise. https://www.florencewise.com/florence-neighborhoods.html

Florence tour: *The 10 most beautiful churches to see in Florence.* (n.d.). https://www.emotionsinflorence.com/blog/important-churches-in-florence.html

Harvey, L., & Marchetti, S. (2024, January 2). *21 best Florence restaurants, picked by a local.* Time Out Florence. https://www.timeout.com/florence/restaurants/best-florence-restaurants

Istituto Il David, Florence, Italy - *Italian courses.* (n.d.). https://www.languagecourse.net/school-istituto-il-david-florence.php3

Jupe, G. (2023, June 12). *11 best places for gelato in Florence right now.* Time Out Florence. https://www.timeout.com/florence/restaurants/best-gelato-in-florence

Luxury Hotels Guides | 5 *star Best Luxury Hotels.* (n.d.). https://www.luxuryhotelsguides.com/

Marchetti, S. (2023, March 5). *Where to Stay in Florence: the City's Best Neighbourhoods.* Time Out Florence. https://www.timeout.com/florence/travel/where-to-stay-in-florence

Nast, C. (n.d.). *Cantinetta Antinori — Restaurant Review* | Condé Nast Traveler. Condé Nast Traveler. https://www.cntraveler.com/restaurants/florence/cantinetta-antinori

Officina Profumo-Farmaceutica di Santa Maria Novella. (n.d.). *Officina Profumo-Farmaceutica Santa Maria Novella since 1221 Florence.* Officina Profumo-Farmaceutica Di Santa Maria Novella. https://uk.smnovella.com/

Scuola di lingua italiana a Firenze - Italia | *Istituto Europeo*. (2018, December 28). Istituto Europeo. https://www.istitutoeuropeo.org/it/

Smith, &. M. (n.d.). *Best boutique and luxury hotels in Florence* | Mr & Mrs Smith. https://www.mrandmrssmith.com/destinations/tuscany/floren ce/hotels

Sohn, K. (2019, December 4). *Rooftop bars Florence.* CN Traveller. https://www.cntraveller.com/gallery/rooftop-bars-florence

The British Institute of Florence. (n.d.). *Home* - the British Institute of Florence. https://www.britishinstitute.it/en

THE TOP 10 Art & Culture in Florence (w/Prices) | Viator. (n.d.). Viator. https://www.viator.com/en-GB/Florence-tours/Art-and-Culture/d519-tag21910

Tripadvisor. (n.d.-a). *Cooking classes in Florence* - Tripadvisor. https://w ww.tripadvisor.co.uk/Attraction_Products-g187895-t12034-zfg11868-a_contentId.42697357624+677460471-Florence_Tuscany.html

Tripadvisor. (n.d.-b). *THE 10 BEST Cafés in Florence (Updated 2024)* - Tripadvisor. https://www.tripadvisor.co.uk/Restaurants-g187895-c8-F lorence_Tuscany.html

Tripadvisor. (n.d.-c). *THE 10 BEST Classes & Workshops in Florence (Updated 2024).* https://www.tripadvisor.co.uk/Attractions-g187895-A ctivities-c41-Florence_Tuscany.html

Tripadvisor. (n.d.-d). *THE 10 BEST Dinner Restaurants in Florence (Updated 2024).* https://www.tripadvisor.co.uk/Restaurants-g187895-zfp58-Flo

rence_Tuscany.html

Wikipedia contributors. (2023a, December 26). *Florence*. Wikipedia. https://en.wikipedia.org/wiki/Florence

Cooke, C. (2020). *Glam Italia! 101 Fabulous things to do in Florence: Insider Secrets To The Renaissance City.*

Plumridge, N. (2019). *Lost in Florence: An Insider's Guide to the Best Places to Eat, Drink and Explore.* Hardie Grant.

10

Conclusion

Printed in Great Britain
by Amazon

36764375R00056